FINISHING THE HAT

The Illustrations of Bill Nelson

FINISHING THE HAT

The Illustrations of Bill Nelson

Text by Bill Nelson

With Foreword by Harry Stein

Editor: Moira Saucer

Designer: Ken Cook

Production Coordinator: Don Beville

Printed in the United States by

Taylor Publishing Company, Dallas, Texas

Finishing The Hat
©1986 Bill Nelson

Taylor Publishing Company
1550 West Mockingbird Lane
Dallas, Texas 75235

Library of Congress Catalog Card Number: 85-090-355

ISBN 0-87833-565-X

An Iron Gate Publishing Foundation Title

To Linda

Acknowledgments

A very special thank you to Stephen Sondheim whose wonderful music and lyrics in his Pulitzer Prize winning musical *Sunday In The Park With George* inspired me to express myself through writing...and for graciously allowing me to reprint the lyrics to "Finishing The Hat." For this honor I also want to thank Arthur Valando, of Tommy Valando Publishing Group and Flora Roberts, Mr. Sondheim's agent. • In the "above and beyond the call of duty department" I want to thank the following: Ken Cook who created a beautiful book around my drawings; Don Beville for his tireless work and his belief in this project; Craig Mattox at Lanman Dominion for all of the color separations (you have always made me look good); Moira Saucer for making all the words I scrawled make sense; Bobby Riddick, Cathy Stone and Anne Argenzio of Riddick Advertising Art for all the fine typography and camera work; Mike Pocklington and Pat Edwards who own very good cameras; Kelly Alder for the art deco page folios; Lu Matthews for the airbrush work on the book title; and my old friend Harry Stein. What can I say, Harry? • In the "support and inspiration department" I want to thank my wife, Linda, who is always there; Kirk Brady who encouraged me to rewrite half of my book; and Vicki Timmons who encouraged me to give it a shot.

THANKS

Contents

Finishing The Hat	9
Foreword by Harry Stein	10
Introduction	16
Clown	19
Call '80	26
Time-Life Records	30
Newsweek	38
Treemonisha	44
Style Moderne	46
The Washington Post	50
Sweeney Todd	54
Man Of A Thousand Faces	58
Hammett	60
Winged	63
Pinheads	66
The First	68
The Actor	70
Animals	72
The Jugglers	78
Old Enough To Know Better	81
Chair Antics	84
Rocking Roy	87
Lavender Shirt	90
Trenchcoat	93
Joseph And The Amazing Technicolor Dreamcoat	95
Maryland Institute College Of Art	98
Red Hot And Cole	104
Dummy	108
Shoeshine	112
Mother Of Exiles	116
Death Of A Salesman	120

Finishing The Hat

Finishing the hat
How you have to finish the hat
How you watch the rest of the world from a window,
While you finish the hat.

Mapping out a sky
What you feel like planning a sky
What you feel when voices that come through the window, go,
Until they distance and die
Until there's nothing but sky.

And how you're always turning back too late from the grass
    and the stick and the dog and the light...

Dizzy from the height
Coming from the hat,
Studying the hat
Entering the world of the hat
Reaching through the world of the hat like a window
Back to this one from that
Studying a face
Stepping back to look at a face
Leaves a little space in the way —
Like a window

But to see, it's the only way to see...

However you live there's a part of you
Always standing by
Mapping out a sky.

Finishing a hat
Starting on a hat
Finishing a hat
Look I made a hat
Where there never was a hat.

"Finishing the Hat" from the Broadway musical *Sunday in the Park with George.* Music and lyrics by Stephen Sondheim © 1984 Revelation Music Publishing Corporation and Rilting Music, Incorporated. A Tommy Valando Publication.

Foreword

What, I wondered, was I doing here? How had I
managed to end up, of all places, in Richmond, Virginia? I
mean, yeah, on the one hand I knew: this friend of mine and
some friends of his were in the process of launching something called the *Richmond Mercury*, and my friend had been
kind enough to vouch for my abilities as a writer-editor. I
did need the job. In the year since
my graduation from jour-
nalism school I had not,
God knows, turned up
anything better.

But still…
Richmond? Gazing about
me after a mere hour and a
half in the burg, I was all but
ready to head home to New York. It was a July afternoon of
blast furnace heat, the kind that otherwise only turns up in
movies starring Johnny Weismuller, and in self-protection
I had confined myself to my air-conditioned car. But what I saw
through the windshield, from the elegant mini-plantations
of the West End to a sleepy, decaying downtown where
everything seemed to move at a crawl, was even more alien
than the climate. It being the summer of 1972 and I being
a rather passionate young man, every bit as unkempt as any
other veteran of what was then being called the New Left,
I could hardly imagine a less hospitable environment than
this courtly, defiantly conservative capital of the Confederacy.

When I finally got myself over to our offices
for my initial meeting with my editorial colleagues, I was
hardly reassured. Like myself, recent graduates of fancy
colleges, they were as new to the business of creating a
publication as I; and even those locally born seemed, from
their politics to their personal style, somehow out of sync
with the place.

Then I became aware of the guy sitting in a cubicle

around the corner from the newsroom, head down, scribbling away.

"Who's that?" I asked someone.

"That's the staff artist."

I walked over and peered over his shoulder. He was putting spectacles on Mickey Mouse.

"Hi. I'm Harry Stein."

"Bill Nelson." He grinned. "I'm very pleased to meet you."

I was instantly struck by the face. The guy looked — no exaggeration — like he was fourteen years old. "Yeah. Well, I'm pleased to meet you, too."

"Welcome to Richmond. It's really not a bad place, once you get used to it."

"No, I'm sure it isn't."

"This Nelson guy," I asked someone back in the newsroom, "how old is he?"

"He's gotta be older than he looks. He's married."

"Married?" I didn't know a single soul of my generation who was married; I'm not sure I even knew anyone who believed in marriage. "Where," I asked, "did you find him?"

"He's from Richmond. He went to VCU, just a few blocks away."

"Is he any good?"

"Very."

"What can he do?"

"Everything."

I am, in case it is not already clear, a skeptic, and I tend to take assertions like this with lots of salt. But the following weeks — a period marked by confusion and pressure and endless labor, as we struggled to give our infant paper style and spirit — opened my eyes about a lot of things. The *Mercury* staff, it turned out, was as talented a bunch as I have ever worked with — and I have since worked at a couple of formidable-sounding national publications. In the last dozen years, several of my Richmond colleagues have, indeed, made rather large names for themselves. But the baby-faced guy in the cubicle off the newsroom was very likely the best of us all.

I found out just how valuable a resource Nelson was going to be the day I completed my article for the inaugural issue. It was on shoplifting—a pasttime that had lately taken on the dimension of sport locally — and it was one of those pieces that seem impossible to illustrate in any but the most obvious manner; say, a photo of a guy in handcuffs, or a sketch of a shady character stuffing something inside his shirt. But Bill gave the cliché a terrific twist. He had *his* shady character lean against a column of type—and extend an impossibly long arm across several other columns to swipe my byline.

As a worker, Nelson proved tireless—and he had to be. Early on, most of the other writer-editors reached the same conclusion I had that first week; that, while the staff photographer's stuff never added much to a piece, the staff artist was a magician. If you needed a complex city scene, or a caricature of a local politician, or a straightforward portrait, or something full of abstractions, or whatever you damn pleased, you'd simply have to enter that cubicle, describe what you had in mind, cajole a little, and a day later there it would be—only better than you'd imagined it.

This last was key. It was not merely the diversity of the work that was striking, or even its technical quality, but the fact that, as he was meeting the requirements imposed on him by us crazies, he managed to make each piece uniquely his own; so much so that pretty soon the entire publication, ever longer on illustration and shorter on photos, reflected the Nelson sensibility.

To be sure, Bill himself was less than entirely thrilled by the enormity of his burden; his salary was, I think, a fat hundred and a quarter a week. But, then, he had created his own problem. Even after a new photographer was hired, we all wanted Nelson's stuff beside our words.

I used to love to listen to Bill gripe about the injustice of it all. (In Richmond, one takes one's amusements where one finds them.) You see, he's the sort of guy who, even when he thinks he's angry, is so unnaturally pleasant about it that you begin to suspect that he doesn't really understand the concept at all. So Bill's towering rages tended to consist of a lot of 'Darn its' and small grins instead of large ones. (He informs me, by the way, that this book will include descriptions of some of his most exasperating professional experiences. This I can't wait to read — Nelson spewing venom all over the page.)

ut mild as he is, and as understated, Bill has always known how good he is. And had a pretty good idea of where he has wanted to go. For in his unassuming way, the guy has been relentless, both in his determination to get his work out to an ever larger audience and in his commitment to self-improvement.

From the start, I have been particularly struck by this last. In a world as comfortable with mediocrity as this one — a world in which not only is rigor no longer a prerequisite to success but can actually be a liability — Bill has never demanded less of himself than the maximum.

During the *Mercury* period, he was just getting started in airbrush. Looking over his stuff, I would routinely be much impressed. I mean, it looked *great* to me. But Bill would merely offer me an indulgent smile. "No, it isn't very good. But it will be."

And by now, he talks about the stuff he was doing for the paper — all of it — the way I might talk about my first laborious effort at constructing a sentence in the second grade.

It was intriguing, as we came to know each other, to note how the qualities so evident in his work found their reflection in his life outside the office. Bill and I were about

as different as a pair of male Americans of the same generation could possibly have been—myself, a jaded, Jewish New
Yorker, ever anxious to sow another wild oat; Bill, a teacher
of Sunday school, madly in love with his wife—but we
rapidly became fast friends because we shared a couple of
very basic assumptions: (1) that the other could be endlessly relied upon and (2) that, though life demands a certain
sense of purpose, it is, all in all, a rather bizarre proposition.
The Bill and Linda Nelson abode may have looked pretty
much like neighboring houses in Richmond, but it probably housed a larger collection of the curious and the arcane
—much of it associated with the silent horror-master Lon

Chaney, Sr.—than any other building in town. Where else
within a fifty mile radius could one find a print of the Todd
Browning classic 'Freaks'? What other local Nixon voter
had decorated his home in early Mickey Mouse?

A word on Bill's lamentable Nixon connection is,
I suppose, in order. Nelson did not often talk politics, and
for a long while I assumed he was as liberal as everyone else
in our office. We were, after all, one of the very few publications in the Commonwealth of Virginia to endorse George
McGovern that fall—and throughout the campaign, Bill's
illustrations of Nixon were delightfully arch. In fact, it was
only on Election Day itself that he casually dropped that
he was voting for the fellow.

I was positively staggered. "But, Bill, how could
you have drawn that stuff if you *like* him?"

He, in turn, seemed taken aback by the question. "My
personal feelings are one thing. My work is another."

Barely a year after the *Mercury* was launched, Bill
was recommended to the art director of *New Times* magazine
by Frank Rich, another veteran of the Richmond venture
and today the drama critic of the *New York Times*. This was
his first national exposure, but it surprised none of us that
he soon became the illustrator appearing with the greatest

frequency in that magazine's pages; or that, shortly thereafter, he was turning up regularly in other national publications. "Luck," as Branch Rickey used to say, "is the residue of design."

Not that Nelson has ever made it easy on himself. His steadfast refusal to abandon Richmond, while very much in keeping with his character, has been, in a pragmatic sense, loony; New York art directors know of the place only by rumor and much prefer to employ illustrators who are within messenger-distance. Taken in this light, Bill's success on the national scene is all the more impressive. But not having been seduced myself by the charms of his hometown, I, for one, can summon up little sympathy when he moans about twenty hour deadlines and the vagaries of the overnight delivery services. Hell, if they're so tired of such problems, there's plenty of room for the Nelsons in my neighborhood.

That would be nice. In point of fact, I see Bill almost never these days; have not, indeed, gazed upon that furry face since a *Mercury* reunion back in '82. We lead very distinct lives, nowadays rarely tread even the same professional ground. But — though the thought would never have crossed my mind back at the beginning — what we have always had in common is not so much specific interests as values. And friends like that are rare indeed.

So, in lieu of seeing Bill, I incessantly rediscover our bond in his work. Every time I spot a Nelson illustration, I am reminded of the qualities that make the man so special — not just talent, but perseverance and bottomless humanity.

Yeah, yeah, naturally I'd rather see Bill himself, at least occasionally. But, see, for that I'd have to go back to Richmond.

— Harry Stein

Donna Ferrato

Harry Stein has written the "Ethics" column for *Esquire* **magazine for many years. "Ethics" proved so popular that the columns were compiled into a book,** *Ethics and Other Liabilities.* **Stein has also written the novel** *Hoopla* **and he is now working on another novel about growing up male in America. He is contributing writer to many magazines.**

Introduction

My illustrations have always explored the human form and the way light accentuates and bathes it. Dramatic lighting, such as stage lighting, enhances the figure and the clothing, creating great contrasts between light and dark, which are very important to my drawing. The light creates emotion and life on a two-dimensional stage. When individual forms are lit properly, they intrigue me. I can become totally absorbed with an elbow or a shoe, forgetting there is more to illustrate before I'm through. • Stage lights highlight and accentuate the planes of the head in the most amusing ways with lighting combinations that are practically infinite. Whereas sunlight often provides harsh contrasts and little fine variation between light and dark, stage and artificial lighting reveal many more subtle gradations between the two extremes. • As a result, the theatre has very much influenced my work. When I watch a play, I am seeing it in two ways, both as an entertainment and art form and as inspiration for my illustrations. It is such a rich reference file! The images and the lights and shadows change before your eyes continuously, offering endless new ideas and revelations. Sometimes when a play is over, I find that from the beginning to the end I didn't move at all, wanting to see everything. • Thus, the actor becomes an integral part of my two-dimensional stage. The light separates the actor from the darkened audience as if he exists on a different plane. The stage images embodied in the actor's presentation become powerful illustrative ideas. • Stage make-up is critical to my work also. The figures I draw all wear simple make-up that I design to convey drama, character, warmth, and emotion. If any of these elements is

Some of the tools of the trade in the theatre. Many times actors fill these little travelling make-up studios with anything and everything in order to be fully prepared. But the main ingredient that makes it all believable, causes it all to come to life, is the stage lights. It's as if the make-up kit is incomplete without the finishing touch.

missing then I cannot draw the subject. My color combinations vary, but basically they tend toward the lavenders, blues, and greens. My color palette is also influenced by the German expressionists, who used garish color to show strong facial emotion. The German artists rendered faces that expressed fear or sadness or degradation, but I try to make mine warm and sensitive, believing there is more than one way to understand the human spirit.   •   Costuming is essential. I like the clothing in my drawings to take on a special life all its own rather than to cover up something. The way clothing drapes a figure is important. Lights do wonderful things to folded fabrics, while wrinkles are expressive. The overlapping layers give heightened interest to the figure. Drapery in statues forever fascinates me, as the folds are so real and powerful. Wrinkled and stretched fabric creates a tension integral to my figure studies. I take care in costuming since an improper costume can ruin a production.   •   Production design, finally, is as important in illustration as it is in the theatre. There is no way to make a play successful without proper staging. This same principle holds true for my illustration. When people ask if I am an illustrator *or* a designer I respond that I am both. The illustrator must provide a proper set design (i.e., format) within which his subject can exist. In addition, the entire plane of the drawing must be prepared for the figure, just as the stage must be dressed and furnished for the actors. There is no way to separate illustration and design. I am a set designer on my flat stage, and I must complete an environment, or I have not completed the task. Even the framework of the figure and the application of the figure require design.   •   Lighting, make-up, set design — they are all considerations in my drawing process. In fact, I was inspired to write a book on my work as a result of seeing the Broad-

The first national magazine illustration I ever did. The client was *New Times* magazine. Excited and scared, I kept thinking that this would be the start of something big. Finally, the beginning of my career. I worked hard. But I worked too light. When the drawing ran in the premier issue of *New Times,* there was no recording tape. It was too pale and had dropped out completely. So much for my career, I thought. Not an auspicious beginning. Another little letdown on the road to a new technique.

way musical, *Sunday in the Park with George.* In that work, Stephen Sondheim sketches the life of the neo-impressionist French painter Georges Seurat as he works on his now-famous canvas *A Sunday Afternoon on the Island of La Grande Jatte.* This show resembles a beautifully composed canvas put to music, with its many levels of color, light, and design. • Sondheim addresses so many problems that face the artist in *Sunday in the Park with George* that I feel the work might have been written for me. The unique, often frustrating, view of the world with which artists seem to be blessed or cursed is there in the exhilarating music. • I had to express myself somehow. Not long after I heard the music, I began to write this collection of backstage views explaining what goes on in my little theatre. I've left the scaffolding up around the images so you can inspect the make-up, the lights, and the props.

Clown

When I was thirteen years old, I saw a film called *The Unholy Three*, starring Lon Chaney, Sr., known to moviegoers of the 20s as "The Man of a Thousand Faces." Generally known for his grotesque creations in *The Phantom of the Opera* and *The Hunchback of Notre Dame*, Chaney set himself apart from his contemporaries through his ability to understand suffering and to convey the perseverance of the human spirit in all its pathos, joy, and physical pain. He breathed life, substance, and believability into his thousand faces. • The son of deaf mute parents, Chaney came to understand, at an early age, the suffering which arises from the ignorance and insensitivity of others. The art of pantomime became his way to communicate his daily experiences to his parents. Before long, he became proficient in communication through body language, recognizing that his body had volume and occupied space. He used that knowledge of volume, light, and make-up to complete his illusion. Little did I know back in 1959, as I sat transfixed watching this man, that his many talents would have a profound effect on my future as an illustrator. • Ten years later, I began my professional career. My early work consisted mainly of pen and ink and wash drawings, lots of cartoons, and caricatures. Since this early work was for a newspaper, everything I did was in black and white. My color sense would develop later. • Eventually, I began to do advertising illustrations, and I then used the pure, unmixed colors right out of Dr. Martin's bottles, modeling them with colored pencils. I chose colored pencils because they were dry, no water colors to streak or run, nothing to spill or knock over, no oil to drag my shirt sleeve impatiently through before the pieces dried. Pencils were clean and immediate.

An example of early work. The background flesh color was airbrushed as were the cheeks. The rest was executed in Prismacolor pencil. I used this as a sample to send to *TV GUIDE*. It was intended to show my ability to draw faces and the accompanying letter stated that. They returned the slide with a note saying they were not interested in using it and reminding me that Jack Nicholson was a movie star and *TV GUIDE* dealt only with television. It's times like that when you want to reconsider your chosen path. This kind of illustration was leaving me cold. I needed more depth in my work. I wanted it all to say more.

Although I continued to do caricatures, advertising illustrations, and cartoons for years, I felt something was missing. My illustrations didn't say anything about me. All of my drawings and caricatures were merely masks hiding my true identity. I felt as if I were heading down a dead-end street. I felt there was more to caricature than a big head and a little body. Advertising art was leaving me cold. Clients had become increasingly disappointed with my finished product, and so was I. Despite my dissatisfaction, I wasn't consciously searching for a new direction.   •   Re-enter Lon Chaney, Sr. My wife had given me a book on old movies for Christmas. Thumbing through it, I spied a wonderful photograph of Chaney, as a clown, in a film entitled *He Who Gets Slapped*. Chaney plays the part of a broken-hearted lover who joins the circus to hide his sadness behind the clown make-up. For some mysterious reason, I went out and bought a piece of brown matte board and began interpreting this photograph with Prismacolor pencils.   •   I began this project during a nine-month period in which I had no work at all. After I got over the fear and the "Lady Sings the Blues" blues, I resolved to do something for myself. If work wasn't going to call me anymore, then I needed to make this time count for something.   •   As I began to draw, I realized what I had wanted to do all along. I wanted to accomplish with my illustrations what Chaney had accomplished on the screen, the exploration of light and the study of the figure in terms of volume and space. Becoming interested in the face behind the mask, the sadness under the painted smile, I wanted my drawings to be warm and elegant, conveying my own feelings.   •   I love

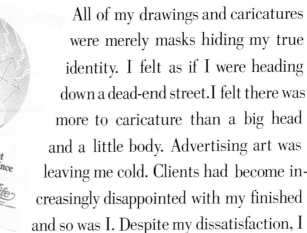

This is an example of the kind of burlesque/caricature I was capable of on a good day when most everything I was doing was disappointing me. I like this little drawing but it couldn't hold my interest for long. My attention span for this type of thing was growing shorter and shorter.

A characteristic pose of Lon Chaney Sr., in clown make-up and costume. This kind of fantastic reference made me feel as if I just couldn't miss. There was only one direction left open to me...up! More feeling, depth, color, and expression! Lights! Cameras! Action!

Prismacolor pencil on Crescent mat board

Prismacolor pencil, rubber stamps on Crescent mat board

the period of the 20s and 30s, so it is not surprising that this period became my main source of reference material. The whites seem to glow, and the photographers do wonderful things with light, rendering faces in dramatic theatrical lighting which gives great strength and feeling to the faces. That world appears to be one occupied by gentle people who are sometimes sad but who are always very human and warm. The photographs recall a simple time and place. Things seem easier. Light is different. Faces are more relaxed and soft. Clothes look more comfortable and classier. Shoes and neckties are marvelous and shiny. I wanted to capture in my drawings the atmosphere, the texture, and the emotion of this time.   •   The world of theatre and make-up has always interested me, especially the way theatre lights illuminate a face. It was this aspect of light I began to incorporate into my drawings.   •   As I worked on the drawing of Chaney, I proceeded with great love and care, qualities that had been lately absent from my work. A change was taking place.   •   As *Clown* progressed, I realized that a layer was burning away. A new direction was coming…and fast. I had resolve. My drawings would be for me. They would be warm, experimental, conceptual. I would explore light, as it bathed faces, causing contrast, obliterating detail, light that glowed, figures occupying space (my space) and having mass. These thoughts washed over me as I worked on *Clown*. Although this seemed to happen in the twinkling of an eye, the groundwork had been laid long before this moment. Ideas, thoughts, and interests were simply converging.   •   My increasing dissatisfaction with my work had weighed heavily upon me and finally broken the camel's back.   •   *Clown* was an immediate success. That year I won my first silver medal from the Society of Illustrators, and many other accolades poured

Prismacolor pencil on Crescent mat board/from the collection of Suzanne and Kevin Chadwick

in. *Clown* had done it, and all of this attention forced me to continue in this vein: I had shown everyone what I could really do, and from now on all would expect the same high standard from me. • I wasn't going to let them, or me, down.

Call'80

The photograph I found in an old book which served as the basis for the main figure in the drawing. I removed the cat and added the little hand puppet.

In 1980 when the Art Directors Club of Richmond asked me to do a call-for-entries poster for the Addy Awards, the local advertising awards show, I decided to try my new technique on the advertising population. • I began my search for appropriate imagery, and I soon found an old photograph of a man in a top hat, wearing a trenchcoat and holding a little kitten. This elegant gentleman would become my central image. I replaced the kitten with a pink puppet, making a personal statement on awards banquets. Some people take them very seriously, an attitude appropriately represented by the gentleman in the top hat. However, others see these functions as mostly an enjoyable chance to get together with their friends and peers. With the little grinning puppet, I signified these folks. • Choosing images that related in some way to the main image and the puppet, I placed the images on a grid background to contrast the involvement and detail of the trenchcoat and head. The man appeared more secure in his space with the grid around him. Prior to beginning this poster, I had discovered rubber stamps as an art form and had wanted to try them out. This grid also made the stamps and other diagrammatic material more logical. Instead of simply floating in space, they now had a sense of incorporation into the whole of the drawing. • I didn't know then that the grid and the small diagrammatic drawings, symbols, and notations would remain with me for many years. The small transparent elements floating near a solid image have become a part of my style, providing a behind-the-scenes view of the

A small rubber head called "The Man of a Thousand Faces" purchased from Johnson Smith and Company years ago. In order for him to display his "Thousand Faces" you have to stick your hand in the back and stretch him out of shape. Too much work. I chose to use the standard face he came with as the model for the hand puppet.

ELBOW GREASE

Rubber stamps which I used on the illustration. I was brand-new to rubber stamps at this point, and it took days and days of deliberation before I would find the nerve to stamp each one on my drawing. After this tenuous beginning I began my own rubber stamp company called Elbow Grease with two friends.

Prismacolor pencil, rubber stamps on Crescent mat board

actual drawing, letting the viewer observe my thought processes and see how I construct a drawing. • This need to leave the scaffolding and building elements up around the newly-built drawing could arise from my need to explain to the world why I draw this way. Obviously, these design elements, which contrast, complement, and enhance the main image, really explain nothing. • The design for *Call '80* pleased me because it looked different from anything I had seen before. But it was not until after I asked my wife if it were complete that I decided it was indeed complete. • The Art Directors Club of New York must have thought so too because that year they awarded me a gold medal for *Call '80*. I also received my second silver medal from the Society of Illustrators, garnering a full-color page in Communication Arts Magazine's *Illustration and Photography Annual*. • *Call '80* advanced my career measurably. After it began to appear in the annuals, I started to receive letters from all over the country requesting copies of the poster. Unaccustomed to so much flattery, had it not been for my insecurity, I probably would have marched right out and bought a new hat in a slightly larger size!

Another example of basically the same design concept as the *Call '80* poster created four years later. The idea of a lone figure on a grid, surrounded by visual material such as rubber stamps and diagrams, intrigues me. The figure becomes very powerful and any function the figure is performing becomes heightened. The attention of the viewer is rivetted to the single bold image. "Keepers of the Light" is the title of this drawing and it was produced as a poster about German optics. The client was Palmer Paper Company who was introducing a new line of German paper and this drawing was one in a series of posters pertaining to this German paper and created by Loucks Atelier out of Houston, Texas.

Some of the diagrammatic influences that helped to shape my style of using small numbers and letters around my figures. Of course, da Vinci had all his numbers and letters backwards so they would read correctly in the mirror!

Prismacolor, airbrush, transfers and rubber stamps on Crescent mat board/from the collection of Suzanne and Kevin Chadwick

Time-Life Records

In 1982, I was commissioned by Time/Life Records to create a series of twenty album covers on the big band era. Perhaps I should explain that I was only asked to do half of the twenty covers planned for the set. The producers may have been concerned that I would get hit by a bus or something and be unable to finish all twenty. At any rate, I had ten album covers to do. Another illustrator, chosen for the remaining ten, gave up on the project after only two covers. During the interim between illustrators, Time/Life considered assigning me all the rest, but I suppose they resurrected their original "careening bus theory" and limited me to the original ten. Eventually, they found another illustrator to complete the set.   •   At the outset, the project seemed relatively easy, and I looked forward to creating these covers. The art director originally expected one album cover every six weeks, giving me enough time between covers to recover.   •   I began with Glenn Miller. Wonderful reference material existed for most of the covers, and this first one was no exception. The Art Deco flavor appealed to me, and I enthusiastically began work.   •   In this business, power shifts often occur in midstream on a project. Time/Life Records was no exception. Before long, the producers had assigned someone else control over the project who gave different directions, different deadlines, and insufficient reference material.

Shortly thereafter, I was asked to provide two covers a month. I complained. Although the reference material got better, the deadlines did not. I was being rushed. I complained again. Surprisingly, the producers listened. The reference material

Prismacolor pencil, india ink on Crescent mat board

Prismacolor pencil, india ink on Crescent mat board

The printed album cover.
I was pleased with the
printing job and I was
surprised to find that the
albums were actually
boxes. The cover was the
top and it hinged to the
left. A nice presentation.

Prismacolor pencil on Crescent mat board

Prismacolor pencil on Crescent mat board

Prismacolor pencil on Crescent mat board

rose again to its original high standards, and they started ask ing me when I thought I could get the next cover to them! Of the ten covers, I chose five to publish here.   •   Not until the album was printed did a friend point out that Glenn Miller's left eyeglass mysteriously disappears behind his cheek. Hmmm. Time/Life never noticed it. Neither did I. Maybe we both need glasses, but we need the kind that go in front of your cheek, not behind it.

I sent this layout up to Time/Life Records to show them how I planned to execute the final draw- ing. They sent it back with all of these interest- ing notes all over it. Plus they added a few color swatches for the border. You never know what's going to come back when you send out a layout. I kept this one because the blue notes actually make an interesting composition.

As a spin-off of these Time/Life album covers, I decided to embark on a whim. I found a photo- graph of these two sing- ers and decided to play with it. After projecting the photograph on my illustration board, I propped up one side of the board, causing the projected image to be- come distorted. The face of the girl became more horizontal. Then I moved things around, elongat- ing the man's face a little vertically. Playing with the images in this way also made me want to do different things with their hair; thus it became clay- like shapes instead of strands. This drawing, done just as an exercise, became a plaything. Her blurred hand suggests a case of nerves, and it fits with her goofy embar- rassed expression. His hand, pointing at the mike, and his weird open mouth look as if he is say- ing "Sing! Now!" The whole thing was so funny. I call the drawing *Opening Night Jitters.*

Prismacolor pencil and airbrush on Crescent mat board

Newsweek

When I began my career I never dreamed I would see my work on the cover of any national magazine, especially *Newsweek*. After all, my father reads *Newsweek*. In 1977, I got a phone call, a request for a cover illustration — my first. Of course, then I thought it was a fluke. They'd meant to call someone else and had accidently gotten me instead. Well, if it were a mistake, then they've made it eight times over the last eight years.   •   It has been a bittersweet relationship to be sure. Seeing my work on the cover of a national magazine thrills me, except, of course, when the work is not my best. In those instances, the week the magazine sits on the newsstand seems like an eternity. Naturally, that issue lingers in the doctor's office for months for all the world to see.   •   These projects are sometimes disappointing because of time limitations. On the average, I have from two to three days to complete a *Newsweek* cover! Sometimes working that fast I turn out something that I detest when it hits the newsstands.   •   Each cover has been a very unique experience. The word *pressure* takes on new meanings during those days of endless work.   •   Here's how the whole process works from *Newsweek's* first phone call to me to the finished cover on the newsstand.   •   When

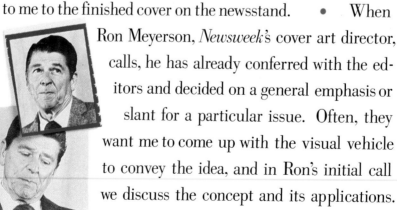

Ron Meyerson, *Newsweek's* cover art director, calls, he has already conferred with the editors and decided on a general emphasis or slant for a particular issue. Often, they want me to come up with the visual vehicle to convey the idea, and in Ron's initial call we discuss the concept and its applications.   •   For the cover I have chosen to show, Ron and the editors had already decided that they wanted a worried-looking President Reagan at the helm of a ship. This idea needed to be worked up into a rough sketch in

The first layout I sent to *Newsweek*. They rejected it because there was too much emphasis on the wagon wheel and too little on Reagan. I really liked this one because of the tension and drama.

The first layout *Newsweek* telecopied to me. This is not as rough as they can get. This one showed me a good deal of what they wanted. It really helped to give me direction.

a matter of hours and then telecopied back to him. Working for *Newsweek*, or any other magazine with a tight deadline, requires the use of a telecopier which transports the image to the client in four to six minutes. • Ron usually wants to see two or three approaches to the subject; consequently, I have produced about three times as many layouts as I have actual covers. • Sometimes the *Newsweek* editors will have a preconceived idea of what they want, so they will telecopy me a sketch first. For this particular cover, they wanted me to come up with an initial sketch, based on their suggestions. • Ron will call after he receives this telecopy to tell me how he feels about it. In this instance, he felt disappointed. As a result, the editors decided to come up with another sketch to provide me with a better idea of what they wanted. • When I received this sketch I saw immediately that they wanted a lighter approach than I had originally tried. So I began again, this time with a better Reagan reference photo from my file. Since I knew that I was finally in the ballpark, I tightened and refined this sketch more than the first. But they didn't like this one either. Ron said Reagan looked too sad and downtrodden. In addition, they wanted me to add a storm-tossed sea and more handles on the wheel. Another sketch from me to them and after an afternoon of waiting, I finally got a go-ahead. This whole stage had eaten up a day-and-a-half, leaving me with the same amount of time in which to execute the finished cover illustration. • Pressure. Increased heart rate. "Why am I in this line of work?" I ask myself. "Why did I have to answer the phone when Ron Meyerson called?" My life flashes before my eyes. As I stare at the blank illustration board, I want to run and hide. • But I got started instead. Many times on a big job, in order to mentally prepare myself for the task before me, I go out to a movie or to

dinner, just to get away from it for a while. All I had now was time for a corned-beef sandwich from the kitchen.   •   As I stated in the first chapter, caricature is not really my strong suit. However, I have been asked many times to do my own brand of caricature, which usually consists of a little body and a big head with few facial exaggerations.   •   In Reagan's case, I could do a fair caricature job because his face is so streaked with wrinkles. The multitude of creases, his turtlelike mouth, his ruddy complexion, his large ears and his hair permitted easy exaggeration on my part. Of course, you might say that I didn't exaggerate anything, and that's really the point. It's not hard to caricature someone whose face is already a caricature to begin with. In retrospect, I think I should have made his hair look more shiny and slicked back. I could have easily added a few white highlights at the lightest points. My favorite parts of his face are the mouth, chin, and eyes.   •   Ten nonstop hours later, I completed the cover, put down my pencils, reintroduced myself to my wife, and took out the trash.   •   At 5:00 a.m. *Newsweek* sent a messenger service to pick up the finished cover and put it on a plane to New York. By 9:30 a.m. *Newsweek* called to say that two things bothered them. They didn't like my rendition of the Captain's hat, and they thought the sky was too dark, but there wasn't time to send the art back to me for revisions. However, *Newsweek* has an art director on its staff, Bob

The final layout. *Newsweek,* late in the day after many meetings, called me with an approval. I was at first relieved and then scared. I always get scared when I do a *Newsweek* cover. So much seems to be riding on it I guess.

Prismacolor pencil, airbrush, water color on Crescent mat board

1.

2.

3.

4.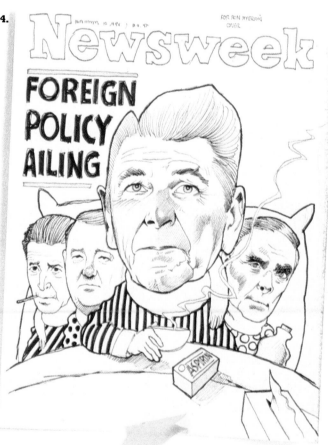

1. This was one of several layouts I submitted during the final weeks of the campaign. There were a million ways to show the three candidates in contention, but since I like puppets, this was my favorite approach. Three little Punch and Judy style puppets with wooden bats battling it down to the wire. *Newsweek* ended up having me do the three candidates hurdling over a voting machine.

Engle, who can imitate any artist's style and who is a fine caricaturist in his own right. Bob went to work on the hat, doing such a perfect job that I didn't even notice it had been changed. The color separator easily changed the sky color by removing some of the black from the black negative. • Even after all this work, there isn't any way for me to know if a cover I have worked on will actually be used until I see it on the newsstand. News changes from minute to minute so I never know when my cover will be bumped for something more urgent. • I usually see the finished cover on the newsstand about three days after I've completed it. After all these years, it's still a thrill no one can diminish.

2. Believe it or not, I'm not sure why I did this particular layout. It may have had something to do with Reagan's ailing foreign policy or the AWACS program or any number of other problems he has encountered. This would have made a great cover.

3. I'm so glad that this layout was never produced as a cover. It was too cutesy and gimmicky. The story dealt with President Reagan's showdown with women on certain sensitive issues. But the idea of a cowboy ("the pres") squaring off against a woman with a six-gun on a Western street and calling it "Reagan at Gender Gap" was just too much. I cringed when I heard the idea. But I went ahead with the layout hoping against hope that somebody up there would see the light.

4. An interesting thing happened on this layout. After *Newsweek* saw it, they told me that it's against policy to show our president in ill health or weak! I couldn't believe it. I thought this was a great idea, but in the twinkling of an eye it was rejected for health reasons.

Treemonisha

In his lifetime, Scott Joplin produced only one opera, *Treemonisha*. Although famed for his ragtime music, he had a burning desire to have this all-black opera produced, but he died without ever seeing it staged. • When Dogwood Dell, a local outdoor amphitheater, decided to produce it for the seventh time since his death, I was asked to create a poster for it. As I started my research, I felt sad that Scott Joplin never got to see the work performed. Deciding that the poster should both reflect a reverence and respect for Joplin and announce this important performance, I wanted my piece to pay tribute to his memory. • Before beginning work, however, I received the unfortunate news that budget problems necessitated the cancellation of the poster. Having heard the music, I had become too involved with the project and too excited about the production to drop the poster idea. I proceeded to create the illustration for the poster in one night, knowing a board meeting had been scheduled for the next day. I suppose my *Newsweek* combat drawing paid off. The board met and immediately approved the poster project. I'm sure some people dug into their own wallets to make the project a reality. • After it was produced, a member of the cast remarked, when she saw the poster, "I wish Scott Joplin could see that." So do I.

Prismacolor pencil, airbrush on Strathmore illustration board

Style Moderne

In the fall of 1981, a small gallery in Richmond hosted my first one-man show. Lots of people came, consuming lots of wine and delivering lots of compliments. The local press responded with good reviews, but the show didn't yield many sales. I recalled the old saying, "You're never a hero in your own hometown," comforting myself with this thought. • The nicest result of that lukewarm emergence into the world of galleries was the poster created especially for the show. I call the illustration *Style Moderne*,

the French name given to the 1930s art movement more commonly known as Art Deco. • A linear, angular look dominates the drawing. The tapestry on the wall, as well as the rug on the stairs, is an original deco design. Even shadows form deco patterns on the wall. I had never drawn anything quite that large in colored pencil before; thus, this was a very ambitious piece for me. Keeping each pencil stroke hidden by the next, and so on, proved especially difficult. • In this early attempt at adding my own colors to a human face, I experimented with strong lights bathing a face. Who is to say what unusual color combinations may result? • The shoes, however, are my favorite part of this drawing. You just can't find shoes like that today anywhere. I made them up. • That poster was the biggest seller at my one-man show. In addition, it did well in all of the national shows, winning a silver medal in the Society of Illustrators show. Shortly after that exhibition, Dai Nippon of Japan contacted me and asked if they could borrow this illustration for a touring exhibition throughout Japan. I com-

Two Japanese publications which published my one-man show poster. It was the first time I had had anything published in Japan.

Prismacolor pencil on Crescent mat board

Prismacolor pencil on Crescent mat board

plied with their request and mailed them the illustration. Looking back, I realize this was a very brave thing to do. The drawing toured Japan for about a year, and I had almost given up on seeing it again when it arrived home safely. The Japanese had taken very good care of it, even reframing it in a better quality frame than I had originally used. In addition, they had published it in their prestigious art magazine, *Idea.* Soon after this, *Idea* contacted me wanting to do a two-page feature on my work in another issue. This kind of reception for an artist is rare. I was really touched by their generosity and by the care they took with my work and the expense they absorbed in shipping, crating, and reframing. • Back to reality. One response to the poster surprised me. Some people who had never met me wondered if this were a self-portrait!

The Washington Post

The *Post* has always been a good client. No, I've never met Ben Bradlee or Bob Woodward or Carl Bernstein (or Dustin Hoffman or Robert Redford for that matter). Mine is a solitary kind of business for the most part. Artists illustrate famous people, but seldom if ever do we meet them. Years ago I published an illustration of Louise Lasser for a *TV Guide* cover. I soon began to receive letters from people wanting to know what Louise Lasser was really like! One man even sent me a sheet of photo-stamps of my cover which he hoped I would forward to Louise since I knew her so well. If memory serves me, he even included a price list in case Ms. Lasser wanted to order more photo-stamps! Unbelievable. • When I draw someone famous, or infamous, it's semi-exciting to think that he or she will probably see my illustration. But, if either does, I never really know because I have never heard from any of my subjects. The case in point with the two *Post* covers I have chosen for this book: I have never met Jack Kent Cooke or Robert Haldeman. • I think illustrators try harder on the portraits of movie stars and politicians, knowing (or hoping) that their subjects might call or write them to say "thanks" for doing a first-rate job. This thought occurs to me each time I illustrate a prominent figure. As a result, I work harder on a portrait of someone living than on someone deceased. • It never occurs to illustrators that these people are always being photographed or drawn; they are accustomed to seeing their faces on magazine covers and posters. We expect them to be as excited as we would be on seeing an illustration of our face on a magazine cover. • I once did a cover for *New Times* which was a portrait of Barbra Streisand completely bald! A friend of mine reported that when she saw it for the first time, she gazed at it for a while and then said, "You know, I don't look half-bad." What a

On the left is the bald Barbra Streisand cover that could have cost me my life had Streisand not liked it. Right, the drawing of Louise Lasser that provoked all of the ridiculous fan mail, all from the Midwest.

This one was printed too light. All of the impact of his head, with all of its wrinkles, was taken away. Left was a pale substitute for one of my better drawings. I was very disappointed. It never seems to get any easier.

Prismacolor pencil on Crescent mat board

Prismacolor pencil on Canson charcoal paper

relief that she didn't hate it.　•　That's what we often content ourselves with—the fact that he or she didn't hate it. No lawyer called. No note attached to a rock hurled through a window. She didn't hate it. Then again, maybe she did but just didn't care.　•　This was the third time I had drawn Haldeman. The first two drawings were for *New Times,* and they didn't paint him in a very favorable light. I felt I owed him one. See how we think—"I felt I owed him one." This is, of course, assuming that he saw the first two. After all, he was pretty busy during the Watergate era when they were drawn. "I felt I owed him one!" Who knows if he even saw the one I owed him?! Anyway, I am very proud of this portrait, whether he saw it or not. Considering my source was a blurred slide, I think I did well.　•　What can I say about Jack Kent Cooke? Perhaps I should confess that since he lives in Virginia, I was certain he would call or write. I even had dreams of selling him the original illustration. Maybe he didn't like the drawing. Maybe he's waiting for me to draw him again because he thinks I owe him one.　•　Maybe he never saw it at all.

The final printed cover got a little dark. What I objected to most were all of the graphic hunks taken out of the drawing by other information. It's sometimes frustrating to have no control over this aspect of the creative process.

Sweeney Todd

Most Virginians know that Barksdale Theatre's Hanover Tavern has witnessed history in the making. Believe it or not, George Washington actually slept there, as well as Thomas Jefferson. Of course, for us natives, this is not a big thrill because those two guys slept all over the place in Virginia. • The Barksdale Theatre has made its own history since staging its first performance in 1953. The first

theatre in the United States to provide a meal prior to the play, Barksdale has staged some daring and ambitious productions, whereas local theatres have settled for more easily produced and popular shows. Often, it is the first theatre outside of New York to purchase the rights to theatrical properties fresh from Broadway runs. • One such play was *Sweeney Todd, the Demon Barber of Fleet Street.* Shortly after it closed at the Uris Theatre on Broadway, it opened at Barksdale. The Barksdale run had the distinct honor of being the only production of *Sweeney Todd* playing anywhere in the U.S. at the time. With music and lyrics by Stephen Sondheim, the play achieved distinction on Broadway, winning the New York Drama Critics Circle Award, a Tony Award for composer-lyricist Sondheim, and a Tony Award for Hugh Wheeler's original source. • At the outset, the Barksdale production of *Sweeney Todd* posed a unique dilemma for the company. A huge, cavernous theatre had housed the Broadway production. How was Barksdale going to feature the work effectively on its small and intimate stage? Luckily, the Barksdale players discovered, to their relief, that Sondheim had originally intended the musical to be performed in an intimate setting. Barksdale not only claimed the first run

A razor used during *Sweeney Todd.* **After the show closed I acquired this razor from Barksdale and painted the title of the musical on the blade in blood red. I presented it to a friend as a Christmas gift. A strange gift but he loved it. He and I both had seen the show six or seven times.**

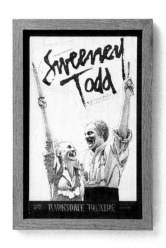

My original pen-and-ink layout which I showed to Barksdale Theatre for approval. I even misspelled Sondheim's name on the layout and they never noticed it; that is, until it was too late. This layout is now part of Barksdale's vast collection of theatre memorabilia.

of *Sweeney Todd* after Broadway, but it also distinguished itself as the first theatre anywhere to perform the work the way the author had conceived it! • Rehearsals were already underway when I entered the project. One visit to the theatre sold me on the power and beauty of this musical. Excitedly, I decided to try to talk Barksdale into allowing me to do a full-color poster for the show. Prior to this, the Barksdale budget had permitted only program covers. *Sweeney Todd* was different. This production demanded special treatment. • After getting the printing and color separations donated, I began the poster design. • Naturally, I wanted to highlight the *personae* of Sweeney Todd and Mrs. Lovett, the charmingly grizzly little woman who baked Todd's victims into meat pies. Additionally, I wanted to capture the frenzied tension at the end of the first act. • Rushing the costume designer into early completion of Sweeney's and Mrs. Lovett's costumes, I staged some photographs. I then went to work, and in a week-and-a-half I had produced the finished illustration. A friend did the calligraphy for me in about fifteen minutes. Using a black magic marker and a paper towel, she skillfully produced the title. I had the rest of the typography set and pasted it, and the poster was printed. • I was pleased with it, and so were the Barksdale folks and the cast and director of *Sweeney Todd.* • Happy ending? No. • Not until after the poster was printed did Gordon Brock ("Sweeney Todd") realize that I had misspelled Sondheim's name! I was devastated. I lost an entire weekend agonizing over it. I recall a friend trying to comfort me, saying, "Who knows how to spell Sondheim anyway?" But I had gotten Sondheim right.

A t-shirt designed by Ken Cook and me for Barksdale. The dripping blood was silk-screened right onto the collar of the shirt and was very effective. These shirts were Christmas gifts from the theatre to the members of the cast of *Sweeney Todd*. I only wore mine out in public once and received so many icy stares that I never wore it again!

I had incorrectly spelled his first name. • Previously, I had hoped this poster might turn some heads on Broadway, but now I felt too ashamed to show it to anyone. Then as the poster began to be distributed around the city, I noticed that no one else seemed to know how Sondheim spelled his first name because no one mentioned it. My confidence began to climb again. • Barksdale's *Sweeney Todd* was a smash hit. We almost got Sondheim himself to come down (and he really wanted to), but he was too busy. Accepted into the Print Casebook's *Best in Covers and Posters*, by the Society of Illustrators, and by the Art Directors Club of New York, the poster turned out a success as well. • Shortly after the play opened, I found an ad agency in New York specializing in entertainment-related advertising, especially in Broadway posters. I sent the art director a *Sweeney Todd* poster, and he called soon after to say how pleased he was with my work. When I told him I had no contacts on Broadway, he said, "You do now." I found out later that he was the art director/designer who created the original Sweeney Todd poster for Broadway! There are many differences in our two approaches, but the main one is that he spelled "Steven" correctly. • Perhaps someday my poster will be worth more because it's an oddity!

Calligraphy created for the poster by Ann Northington. In the course of fifteen minutes she designed this typography using a large black magic-marker and a porous paper towel. The results are bold and graphic and reflect the frenzied energy of the show. I resisted the temptation to print this typography in blood red. I thought it would be too obvious and gimmicky.

Prismacolor pencil, airbrush, watercolor on Crescent mat board/from the collection of David Dunville

Man Of A Thousand Faces

From time to time, I return in my drawings to Lon Chaney, Sr. His facility with light and his myriad expressions captivate and mystify me. He possessed such infinite grace that it's almost as if he were a living painting. • For therapeutic reasons, I draw him again and again. • I based this drawing, *Man of a Thousand Faces*, on a photograph of Chaney wearing absolutely no make-up. He simply used the lights to bring off the mood, a technique which intrigued me enough to use it for the drawing. • I chose canson paper as a background in order to allow the whites in his face to stand out starkly on the darker field of the paper. To complement the already eerie pose, I added lots of ghoulish color to the face. I love to experiment as I go along, adding colors that might not seem to belong on a human face. Since I am always thinking in terms of light sources illuminating my subjects, it's natural to conceive of and accept these colors. There's no limit to my color palette. • My wife dislikes this strange drawing. It's a little too macabre for her.

Two 8 x 10 glossies of Lon Chaney, Sr. Each photo shows the range of emotion he was able to capture. The same kind of emotional power I wanted in my drawings.

A shot of a sad Lon Chaney, Sr. He was able to create great pathos as well as the chilling horror he brought to the screen in *The Phantom of the Opera*.

Prismacolor pencil on Canson charcoal paper

Hammett

Many consider Dashiell Hammett, the detective fiction writer, to be the father of the hard-boiled detective story narrated in the first person.   •   Best known for *The Maltese Falcon* and *The Thin Man*, Hammett apparently lived his own stories, basing his fiction on real-life experiences as a Pinkerton detective. He loved to roam the dark, crowded streets of San Francisco's Chinatown and the waterfront bars and dives, gathering material and inspiration.   •   Suffering from tuberculosis, which took a heavy toll on his health, Hammett kept extremely late hours and drank excessively. His hard-driving lifestyle, in addition to his poor health, caused him to suffer depressions and, consequently, writer's block. He went for months and sometimes years without writing.   •   Besides writing, Hammett participated in many leftist causes, joining the Communist Party, an affiliation which would eventually destroy his public credibility. By January of 1950, the FBI had compiled a detailed report on his political activities spanning a four-year period, linking his name with thirty-five Communist-front organizations. He had proven his loyalty to his country by serving in both World Wars, but he refused to keep silent about the injustices and hypocrisies he perceived.   •   In 1951, Hammett was arrested. After a hearing in which he invoked the Fifth Amendment on more than eighty occasions, he was sentenced to six months in federal prison. Soon after his release, he was blacklisted in Hollywood.   •   The IRS then pressed him with a bill of $111,000 in back taxes. Hammett wrote: "Nothing lasts. You can't count on anything but yourself."   •   After many other setbacks, he suffered a major heart attack in 1955. He was not yet fully recovered when the IRS filed a tax judgment of $140,800 against him, and the New York State Tax Commission billed him an additional $16,000. As one friend put it, "The hounds

were snapping at his heels, but Dash refused to run. He walked proud. He lost a lot—but he never lost his nerve or his pride." • In 1960 he experienced a pain in his shoulder, attributing it to rheumatism. The doctors diagnosed lung cancer, but they never told him. On January 10, 1961, Dashiell Hammett died. The medical examiner stated that the death, due to cancer, was further complicated by emphysema and pneumonia, in addition to bad kidneys and to a diseased heart, liver, spleen, and prostate gland. He weighed 118 pounds. • Congdon and Weed Publishers in New York approached me in 1983 to illustrate a dust jacket for a new biography on Dashiell Hammett. They wanted me to capture in his face the life I have just told you about. His face had to reflect the ravages of alcoholism, tuberculosis, emphysema, mental strain, and general dissipation, while maintaining an air of dignity, pride, strength, and perseverance. The publishers requested these soulfully sad eyes, infused with light and life. • That sounds pretty difficult to achieve, doesn't it? Well, ordinarily I am up for such a task, given the proper reference photographs from which to work. In this case, however, Congdon and Weed had a particular pose in mind, and the photograph they provided captured a young, dashing, healthy twenty-eight year-old Dashiell Hammett! I had to age him about twenty years and who knows how many fifths of scotch. • My knowledge of theatrical make-up usefully provided the principles by which I made him up into a man in his fifties. I had to thin out his face, sink in his cheeks, add bags under his eyes, weaken his mouth and chin, and thin out his hair, while preserving an air of dignity. • The cover turned out okay, but I would hate to see an actual photograph of him at that age. I was only guessing. It's so hard to know how a person will age and what changes will take place. How-

This is the photo Congdon and Weed sent me to work from. Dashiell Hammett was twenty-eight years old and healthy as could be in this portrait. I was amazed that this was all they had but I got right to work aging and thinning him.

ever, his difficult life and the severity of the physical pain and stress he suffered provided abundant clues. • Nunnally Johnson succinctly summed up Hammett's life:"He lived life at the edge, because he saw himself as a man who possessed no future....Hammett had no expectation of being alive much beyond Thursday."

The dust jacket for the Hammett book. I am unable to show the actual drawing because when it was returned to me it arrived folded in half! Looking purely on the "cockeyed optimistical" side of things, I guess I could say that someone decided to age him a litte bit more than my initial attempt. There was a nice crack running right through the middle of his face!

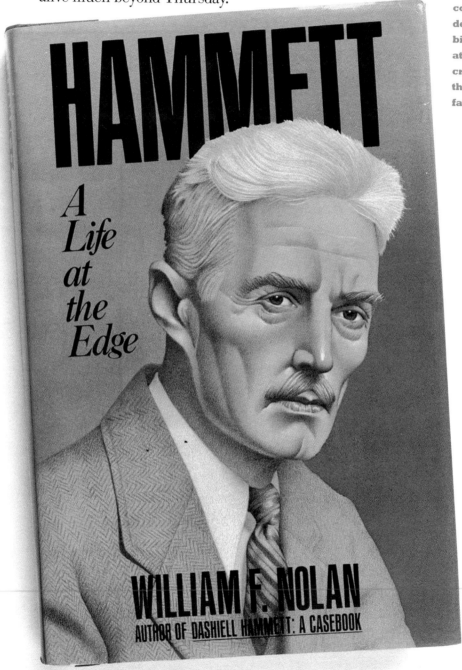

Special thanks to Congdon and Weed Publishers for permission to quote lines from Hammett.

Winged

A purely conceptual piece, *Winged* evolved out of my interest in the majesty and grace of statuary and my love of draped and wrinkled fabric. I used as a reference a female figure situated at the base of a statue in Battery Park in Manhattan. The statue commemorates Giovanni da Verrazano, a man many Italian-Americans claim sighted New York Harbor in 1524 — eighty-four years before Henry Hudson did. This female figure at the base of the statue represents Discovery. • I saw her once in New York and fell in love. The corrosion that had taken place, mainly on her face, fascinated me. The green streaked copper surface added to her aura. • Of course, my all-time favorite, The Statue of Liberty, or as she was originally called, *Liberty Enlightening the World,* stands just a stone's throw away. Awestruck when I see her, I simply marvel that anyone could sculpt something that large and that perfect. Since the Statue of Liberty had been drawn and photographed so many times, I felt my rendering of this incredible woman, Discovery, would yield a fresher opportunity for me to explore my love of statues. • Originally, her arms held a torch and a sword, but I decided to draw her without arms. In my eyes, the arms diminished some of the power I saw in her, seeming unnecessary to the drawing. Instead, I replaced them with wings, but these were wings made of fabric instead of feathers. • I intended to show a figure overcoming or defying its bounds. The grid served to lock the figure in, but her wings unfolded past her perimeters. Not content simply to embody Freedom, I decided to allow her to expand her existence past the edge of the illustration board. Adding another piece of board around the original drawing, I continued her wings, an act totally out of character for me. • Discovery embodies a kind of exhilarating freedom I allowed myself to have with this drawing. She also

Reference photos of the statue in Battery Park that first inspired me to do this drawing. The first time I laid eyes on her, with all of her oxidation and age, I knew that I would eventually have to transfer her to paper. It's almost as if my creating a drawing of her would somehow prolong her life. Of course, a bronze statue can definitely outlive a piece of paper.

Berol #2 graphite pencil on Strathmore illustration board/from the collection of Ann Kern

symbolizes a kind of perseverance to me. She's worn and weather-beaten, but she's still striving. • The small diagram, a rubber stamp of the famous drawing by da Vinci, provides a contrast to the woman's situation. While she moves forward, he remains limited to his environment, fluttering helplessly. It seemed only natural to call this drawing *Winged*. • I drew the piece in graphite pencil, fully intending to render it in color. I soon realized, however, that it was complete in black and white. Color would somehow diminish her power.

Photo reference of a fashion model. The direction and thrust of her raised arms looked like wings to me so I incorporated them into the drawing while removing the arms of the statue. At the time, this process seemed perfectly logical. After all, I was influenced by the majesty of the Statue of Liberty and wanted to create something striking but dissimilar. And of course, the power of the Nice of Samothrace *(The Winged Victory)* was a great influence for removing the statue's arms and adding wings. But they had to be different. My wings.

Pinheads

In Bernard Pomerance's play *The Elephant Man*, Joseph Merrick[*] finds himself restricted to a life of suffering in cold, dark rooms. His horrible disfigurement, the object of horror and ridicule, isolates him so much from others that he has little sense of his intellectual potential and his human possibility. In his small and lonely world, he has no one else with whom to compare himself. • Going off to make arrangements for their travel to another town, his manager leaves him alone one evening. Nearby is another sideshow attraction—two pinheads—also left alone. Pinheads, or severely retarded persons, usually have no more intelligence than that of a small child. • To pass the time, Merrick attempts to strike up a conversation with the two retarded women, who merely babble and giggle. At this juncture, Joseph Merrick has a crucial revelation: he realizes his intelligence. • The haunting image of these two women and what they represented stayed with me after the play ended. Their costumes, the large pointed headpieces, and the wide crinoline collars and cuffs constituted a moving and intriguing image, the possibility for a drawing. The pinheads were beautiful and warm, but they also projected fear and terror. I wanted to capture this complexity of emotion in my drawing. • The drawing came quickly. In this case, as in many others, I became emotionally involved with and excited about my subject matter, and the illustration mirrored that excitement and involvement. Sometimes I become so excited about an image that I can't rest until I have transferred that image to paper. • For some reason I felt more strongly about this one than most, and, as a result *The Pinheads* remains my favorite drawing.

[*]Editor's Note: Although the character's name is "John," the author feels it is more appropriate to call him by his given name "Joseph."

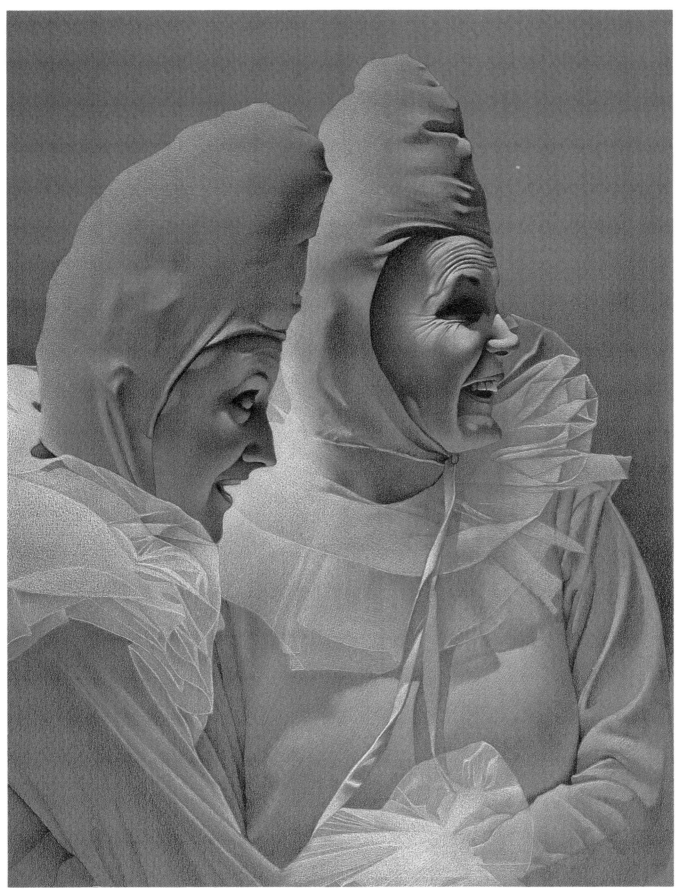

Prismacolor pencil on Crescent mat board

The First

The First, a Broadway musical, traces the career of Brooklyn Dodger Jackie Roosevelt Robinson, the first black man in major league baseball. Exciting times, right? The story held the potential for a wonderful musical, also, but the production died on Broadway after about a month. My idea for the poster didn't even live that long. • A New York advertising agency commissioned me to come up with a comp idea for a Broadway poster for *The First*. A comp is generally a very tight sketch, an almost finished illustration. My first impulse was to design a giant baseball card for the poster. In fact, I was so sold on the idea that I went a few steps further than a comp, and I had the poster typeset, which resulted in a very finished looking piece for presentation. • I was so sure this one was going to be my first Broadway poster, I could taste it. • *The First* was not to be "the first" for me. The idea was rejected. It could have also been "the first" baseball card Broadway poster. • I still believe it could have been a winner.

The Jackie Robinson baseball card that gave me the initial idea to do a baseball card Broadway poster. I still think it was a terrific idea. A gigantic baseball card looming over Times Square. Take down that *Cats* billboard. I continue to dream big.

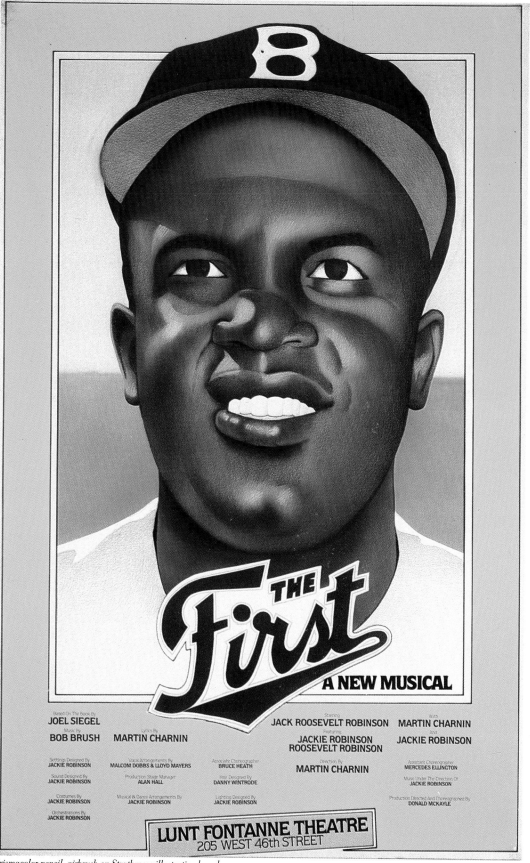

Prismacolor pencil, airbrush on Strathmore illustration board

The Actor

I like the color. That much I like. And I like the shoes, but overall I'm bored by this drawing. It was done as a limited edition, self-promotion for a printer, who faithfully reproduced the drawing. • There's just not enough happening. • Actually, there's nothing happening. • I have become spoiled, accustomed to having more going on in my illustrations. There's got to be some life, something in  there to hold my interest. • The shoes aren't enough, and the color isn't enough. • I show it to you so you'll know what I dislike. And perhaps, you'll say how brave I am to show a piece in my book that I consider a failure. • Well, it's not a total failure. • I do like the color...and the shoes.

This illustration for the Kennedy Center prompted me to do "the actor." The colors I used impressed me so much that I decided that using the same color scheme again on a more interesting subject could only generate a more interesting finished product. There's more to an illustration, however, than a good set of colors.

Madama Butterfly

GIACOMO PUCCINI—1904

In 1900, when Giacomo Puccini was in London to supervise the local premiere of *Tosca*, he was persuaded to see *Madam Butterfly*, the play which David Belasco had successfully adapted from John Luther Long's pathetic tale of a child-like geisha who waits faithfully for her faithless American husband to return. Although he could scarcely understand a word of English, the composer recognized a dramatic situation which could instantly engage the emotions of a sensitive spectator. With unerring theatrical insight, and an irresistible flow of melody, he transformed the play into one of the most beloved of operas. It returns to Kennedy Center in the same production—directed by Francis Rizzo and designed by Ming Cho Lee—which electrified Washington audiences in 1977. John Mauceri conducts a cast including Patricia Wells, Richard Stilwell, Judith Christin, André Lortie and Noel Tyl.

IN ITALIAN
THE OPERA HOUSE
REVIVAL

Prismacolor pencil, airbrush on Strathmore illustration board/from the collection of Bobby Riddick

Animals

In early 1984, an illustrator in Pittsburgh named Jackie Geyer wrote, asking if I would contribute to a collection of illustrations. She had written to various artists asking each for a drawing of a cat. She caught me at a slow time work-wise, so within a couple of weeks I had completed her cat, choosing as my subject the idea that cats hate water. • Shortly after that, a friend in Washington asked me to do an illustration of a rabbit and a camel for his girlfriend, who likes both. I included both, placing the camel in a picnic basket the rabbit carried. • In the spring of 1984, I received a request to design a concert poster. Since the art director had told me that the client wanted me to use animals in the posters, I went to my first meeting armed with my rabbit and camel drawing, which the art director loved. As a result, I created a layout using the same general design as before, but I replaced the rabbit with a mallard duck and the camel with a rabbit, a baby duck, and a clarinet. The Brookfield concerts poster was complete. • Two months later another illustrator from Pittsburgh requested a rabbit drawing. At that point, I realized that Jackie Geyer had never seen another animal drawing of mine. And my friend in Washington hadn't seen the cat drawing when he asked me to do the rabbit and the camel. Finally, the other illustrator had seen only the cat and not the rabbit/camel drawing when he asked me to do the other rabbit. • All of these seemingly unconnected commissions had led to a menagerie, my own zoo. I had discovered the enjoyment of drawing these creatures wearing human clothes and doing human things. The drawings are fresh and spontaneous and very therapeutic. In other

Prismacolor pencil on Canson charcoal paper/from the collection of Paul Schifino

Prismacolor pencil on Canson charcoal paper

"WANNA BUY A DUCK?": JOE PENNER comedian of the stage and radio, who coined the expression, is now making a personal appearance at one of the local picture houses

This shot was used as the basic body with basket for the duck. Sometimes things are so nice that you just can't change them much. So I stylized it a bit and basically swiped it. I guess that's why they call these things *swipes!*

BROOKFIELD CONCERTS

Musical summer evenings on the Lawn at Brookfield — West Broad Street and Dickens Road. All concerts begin at 7:00 p.m.—Free to the public, ample parking and easy access.

June 5 Rain date: June 6
The No Elephant Circus
—A child's delight...the magic of circus arts accompanied by The VCU Summer Serenade Orchestra

July 3 Rain or Shine
Life of Virginia Salutes the USA with the Langley TAC Band—aerial salute by 192nd TAC Fighter Group

July 24 Rain date: July 25
Blackwater
— rocking Country & Western

August 14 Rain date: August 21
Sounds of Scotland
—John Turner & Friends, and the Acca Highlanders

September 4 Rain date: September 5
Chairmen of the Board
— Beach Blanket Bash!

September 18 Rain date: September 19
Delbert McClinton
—red-hot Texas rhythm & blues

The soft, unrich, and unbrilliant layout I submitted for approval to the client. Now that I see how rich and brilliant I made the finished drawing, I'm surprised that they approved it in its original state.

LIFE OF VIRGINIA

NELSON '85

A very faithful reproduction of the original drawing. The typography isn't bad. At first, I didn't like the list of dates obscuring the clouds, but I got used to it. It turned out to be a nice visual communication.

words, they are personally satisfying. Now when there's a slack moment or week or month, I just add some more animals to my zoo. • It's a small zoo. Most of the drawings (except the Brookfield poster) measure about 5″ x 7″. I like the challenge of working in this small framework. I experiment with my animals, trying different pencil techniques and color combinations and dressing them in different outfits. Sometimes I create landscapes and experiment with different skies and cloud formations. • I have big (or should I say small?) plans for a gorilla, a koala bear, and an ostrich. • You can learn a lot from animals.

Prismacolor pencil on Canson charcoal paper

The Jugglers

Sometimes an illustration has to come out of my head before I can rest. When this sort of thing happens, I will get an idea in pieces. I see a face, sense the composition, and then individual elements, such as the flowers and the balls, will materialize. Then I see the key that ties it all together. It could be anything, but in this case, it was the little pieces of paper blowing in from the lower left. • The various puzzle pieces may float around in my head for as long as a month until I actually fit them together in the drawing. Before ever putting pencil to paper, I knew what the finished drawing would look like. I had been rehearsing it for weeks, trying this and that, and endlessly putting different elements together in my mind. • I kept searching for the right combination until one impulse, very new and daring, demanded attention—the idea of creating a drawing that appears to move. Thus, I created the illusion of motion with the standing figure's left hand. Creating motion is like entering another dimension. • With the blowing papers as the missing puzzle piece, I began to construct *The Jugglers.* After so much forethought and planning, I found the actual execution anticlimactic. Having seen it hundreds of times in my mind, I already knew the result. My little, nonsensical, diagrammatic design elements were a must. I already knew where they were going to go. • This particular process doesn't happen every time. In fact, most

The intriguing photograph I found of an early vaudeville team that I decided to use as the basis for *The Jugglers.* The strange thing is that I had seen the whole jugglers illustration finished in my mind before I ever stumbled across this photograph!

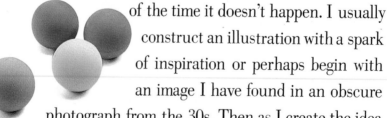

of the time it doesn't happen. I usually construct an illustration with a spark of inspiration or perhaps begin with an image I have found in an obscure photograph from the 30s. Then as I create the idea on paper, I begin to see other possibilities. It's very rare that I begin with a thumbnail or a blueprint of any kind. I just start, feeling the need to let

The sketch used to work out all of the design problems. Believe it or not, I could have almost done this sketch before I found the photographic reference.

Prismacolor pencil, paint chips on Canson charcoal paper/from the collection of Steve Puckett

something out onto the paper and then to embellish it as I go. • This method keeps the adventure of drawing fresh, new, and infinitely interesting. Not sleepwalking through the execution, I experience one thrill after another as new elements and ideas emerge. • Sometimes I become so involved and excited that I don't even want the drawing to be finished. In fact, many times I will reach a point of almost finishing, and I will put the piece up for a few days, in order to permit my mind to regroup and to begin to formulate new additions so I can keep working on it. This is my favorite way to work. • Many people have to begin with a plan, but then, so do I. I begin with the thought that I plan to have a great deal of pleasure creating a drawing from a blank piece of paper.

Old Enough To Know Better

Singer and songwriter John Small asked me to design the illustration for his first album cover. John wanted himself sitting in a bathtub with a rubber duck, apropos considering that he entitled the album *Old Enough to Know Better* and included on it a song called "Fun in the Tub." • The night we had chosen for shooting the photographs from which I would work had to be the hottest, most humid night in Virginia's history. The photographer had, somehow, found an available bathtub in an apartment, and we arrived there around 7:00 p.m. I had shopped around earlier that day and found the perfect rubber duck in an antique shop. I thought we were all set. • The bathroom in this apartment was so small it was hardly there. It became not only a gargantuan task just to fit the lights into the site, but it also proved a time-consuming job to get the lights right. • The temperature in that bathroom had reached about one-hundred degrees by the time we were ready to shoot. In order to climb into the tub (which was also minuscule), John had to climb over the light stands and wires. • The duck posed the next problem. The configuration of John's head, shoulders, and arms prevented John from holding the duck, and we invested considerable labor in rigging up a rod with the duck attached to the top of it so that John could hold it between his knees. Problematically, John's knees would quickly tire from being folded up in front of him for extended periods in that cramped tub. He would have to stand and stretch periodically, meaning he had to tackle the tripod and wire obstacle course again. • Finally, after several preliminary polaroids to check the light, we were ready for the real thing. Before we could start, though, I had to wet

The little celluloid duck that I scoured antique shops to find. In order to have it appear to be a rubber duck I had to eliminate the spring in the drawing. The spring would have rusted in the bathtub.

John Small liked the little duck so much that his wife put it in his Christmas stocking.

John's hair down and lather up some soap in the sink to put on his shoulders and on the duck's head.   •   The sweat soaking John's head proved sufficient for lathering. He was dripping with sweat, as were we all. It was definitely a forgettable experience, but we got a great cover out of it.   •   Looking back, I wonder why we put ourselves through so much. There must have been an easier way. The next time we'll all be "Old Enough to Know Better."

It was the hottest night I can remember. No air-conditioning and those lights heated things up even more. John was rapidly losing weight sweating away in the tub, and that's me on the toilet seat holding a bottle of warm suds.

JOHN SMALL

*Old Enough
To Know Better*

Prismacolor pencil on Canson charcoal paper

Chair Antics

Have you ever felt compelled to do something that might seem strange to everyone else? Well, I have that feeling from time to time. I had it when I conceived of *Chair Antics.* • The inspiration for this drawing began with the bentwood chairs we sit in for meals. Although bentwood doesn't strike me as all that comfortable, I have always liked its artistry and simplicity. I just like to look at it. However, chairs alone do not make an arresting image. • I needed other things going on in the drawing. Since I like to draw figures and since they went so well with the chairs, the two men were naturals. For a long time, I left the drawing with just the men and the chairs. Lacking the deadline of an assignment, I put it aside, as I do often. • I often look at a drawing a long time before completing it. Usually, there comes a point when I don't know where I'm going anymore, so I stop. This is a definite improvement over my previous technique. I used to come to a brick wall and force my way through, coming out on the other side with a rushed, ill-conceived drawing. I learned this new approach after crumbling too many brick walls. • Three or four months had passed when I just decided one night to visit the library to look up Michael Thonet, the creator of bentwood furniture. I was amazed to find not only photographs of all of Thonet's furniture, but also the most beautiful side and front view diagrammatic mechanical drawings of the two bentwood chairs I had drawn. These two diagrams had to be somehow incorporated into the drawing. I added two circles on either side of the standing figure, placing the two diagrams there. But they seemed to float strangely. They needed an anchor, a reason for being. Once a modified grid was added, they made sense. • For some reason, the drawing still looked empty to me. Being fond of letter forms, I decided to write something in the background. I racked my brain for weeks

Wonderful chair reference from my own kitchen. Thonet's graceful lines inspired me to begin by drawing the chairs themselves, and although they are perfectly beautiful by themselves, I felt I needed more. I may have gone overboard but I think I still kept the flavor of the bentwood. I just couldn't leave it as two chairs.

A work-in-progress polaroid taken to study as I very slowly designed and concepted the drawing and felt my way along. This is my normal procedure. Many times I begin uncertain of the concept for the finished drawing. Beginning inspires me to explore different avenues and ideas. If I didn't start with a germ of an idea I would never go anywhere.

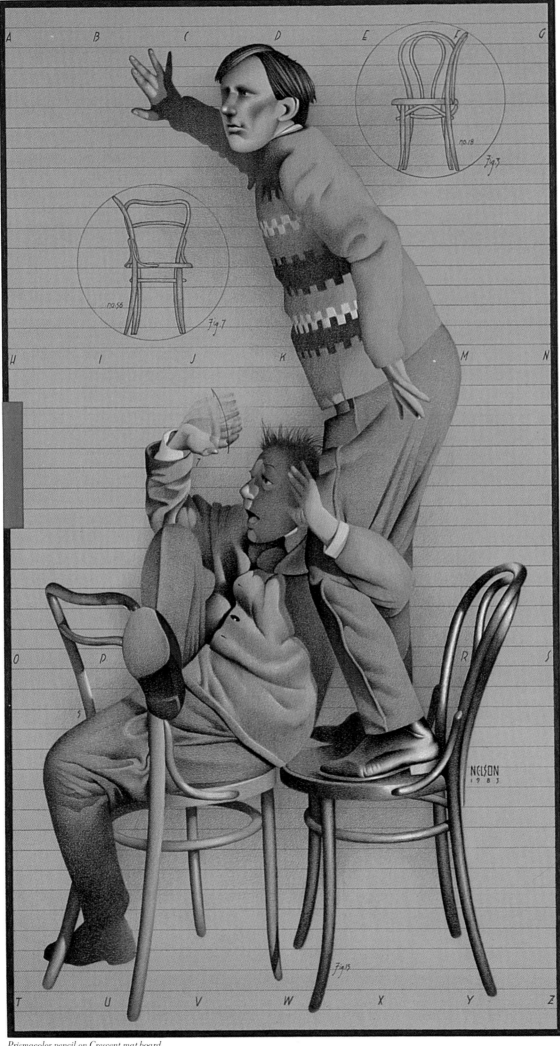

Prismacolor pencil on Crescent mat board

trying to arrive at the right word or phrase to complete the drawing. Nothing. I needed some form of calligraphy to complete the illustration. Since I couldn't think of anything to say, I simply decided to put letters in their purest form around my chair-bound men: the alphabet. It worked. I don't know why, but it worked. • I wish I could explain why I put the piece of red paper on the border. If I said it was to give the guy having the worst time in his chair something to look at, you would think I didn't have all my oars in the water, but that's why. He needed something to see. The standing guy had the diagrams while the seated guy didn't. He seemed to be reacting strongly to something; therefore, I gave him a focal point. He was seeing red. Both of these fellows contrasted so sharply with the grace and beauty of the bentwood chairs, and I liked the resulting tension. The diagrams helped to heighten that tension. I added the hand in motion so I could try my hand (actually his hand) at blurred imagery. *Chair Antics* seemed the perfect title to sum up the final composition. • Perhaps I should have said, "It's just something I had to do" and left it at that.

Rocking Roy

Motion intrigues me and adds another dimension to my illustration. Of course, this is the motion I pretend exists in my drawings, as opposed to motion as it occurs in real life. With modeling and shading, I try to create the illusion of a third dimension; in using motion, I sometimes feel as though I'm tampering with a fourth dimension. The blurred imagery gives additional life and credence to my figures and produces the illusion of action fast enough that only quick pencil movements, blurred, could capture it all. • Creating motion also gives the drawing a harried or unsettled look. This was my intention in creating *Rocking Roy*. The way I saw it, Roy was just sitting backwards in his chair, rocking peacefully and daydreaming, when we came and caught him in mid-rock. Naturally, he would appear a little surprised and, since he was rocking, a little blurred. Disconcerting, right? It's no fun to be shocked out of a nice little daydream. Roy knows. • When I showed this drawing to a friend, he said, "It's pretty good, Bill, but you smeared it when you pulled it out of your portfolio!"

Roy in mid-rock. Disconcerted. Jarred. Caught in a daydream. Motion and emotion. All of these thoughts come to mind when I see *Rocking Roy*. And then Ken Cook said, "Hey, great drawing, but you smeared it when you took it out of your portfolio."

Prismacolor pencil on Canson charcoal paper

Lavender Shirt

Whenever I see a white shirt, I always see the shadowed areas in predominantly lavender hues. Suffering from no illusions, I realize that the lavender probably isn't really there. But it is certainly there in my drawings. It's like saying, "If I can't have reality the way I really want it, then at least I can have it my way in my own drawings." So I draw lavender shirts. I also see, in these white shirts, blues, pinks, and yellows. All of these colors contrast so beautifully with white to bring it alive. • In this particular drawing, the shirt has become the most important part of the composition. The fabric appears to move, alive with beautiful wrinkles and shapes. All of my shirts have to be cotton because cotton wrinkles and creases so wonderfully. As I stated earlier, I become lost in the folds of the material, actually forgetting there are other parts of the drawing requiring my attention. • The secret to a successful drawing partly involves treating each part as a whole and forgetting there is anything else to render. Concentrating all my energy on one aspect of the composition, I accomplish that part to my satisfaction. I forget about time and the rest of the drawing, waiting impatiently to be fleshed out. Naturally, if I complete one area perfectly, I am forced to draw each area as meticulously. • When I look at this drawing, all I focus on is the shirt, despite my careful attention to the head, pants, shoes, and floor. The drawing works well as a whole, but I love that lavender shirt. • Some colors are just favorites, and I want to use them everywhere. I have already stated that I use lavender in faces, but it works best in my white cotton shirts. The stylized wrinkles

Prismacolor pencil on Crescent mat board

and folds give such fluidity, the semblance of beautiful statuary. • This particular shirt simply captivates me. Do you see my fascination, or is it only me? The pants are nice, and I like the head, but that beautifully alive, fluid drive lavender shirt is the only thing I see.

In a drawing of a white shirt, I probably use five or six lavender pencils. It's always been one of my favorite colors. In fact, the guest bedroom in our home is painted lavender. We don't get many guests.

Trenchcoat

I don't know why I drew this. Yes, I do. It's because I like the mass of the coat and the way the fabric hangs. This drawing just happened as I went along. I had no preconceived idea about the finished appearance. • Many of my drawings become exercises in color and spatial studies. In this one, I used this coat and head to explore color. I do this kind of therapy, or personal experimentation, mostly on personal portfolio pieces, as this one is, but I do find myself experimenting in my assignments also. And that's good. The client is rarely, if ever, disappointed when I have tried something new. When I do bring something different to a job, my work keeps me more interested, and my attempt is more alive and fresh. *Trenchcoat* is a little strange, I'll admit, but it's okay since it's for me. You've noticed that he has no top to his head, no hair. In this case, I thought hair would detract from the piece. Besides, I wasn't experimenting with drawing hair differently; I was only dealing with facial planes and fabric. • The little fellow in a trenchcoat is one of my own rubberstamp designs, cut out and colored to match the large figure. One guy in the drawing should have a top to his head, even if it's covered by a hat.

An old ad clipped from a 1920s magazine. I have always loved those huge old trenchcoats they used to wear back then. I decided to go a few light years past that for something fairly dramatic and bizarre. The old ad served as a jumping-off point.

Prismacolor pencil on Crescent mat board

Joseph And The Amazing Technicolor Dreamcoat

Responsible for the award-winning smash hits *Jesus Christ Superstar* and *Evita,* Andrew Lloyd Webber and Tim Rice comprise one of the most talented composer-lyricist teams in the legitimate theatre today. • Their first effort back in 1967 was *Joseph and the Amazing Technicolor Dreamcoat.* Faithfully based on one of the most beautiful stories in the Bible, the musical's wonderful, tuneful songs leave the theatregoer humming and singing for days after the show. • It is a heartwarming, uplifting show. When Barksdale Theatre decided to stage it, I decided that it needed a full-color poster. After attending a few rehearsals, I came up with a concept and a direction. Next, as with the *Sweeney Todd* poster, I rushed the costume designer into early completion of two costumes, Joseph's and the narrator's. I really felt sorry for him. Not only was he the costume designer, but he was also the set designer and make-up artist. I found myself actually hounding him to finish the costumes. At least three people were working on the construction of Joseph's technicolor coat, applying the colors in counted cross-stitch, a procedure which added to the delay. Unable to wait any longer, we finally scheduled a photo session without the completed coat. The costume designer gave me a drawing of the coat in color. • Meanwhile, the narrator's costume presented great problems. Every attempt at construction had failed, and finally we could wait no longer on this costume either. We photographed the narrator in a bathing suit, and I began drawing her head, arms, hands, and shoulders while the costume was still under construc-

The actual needlepoint and satin flight jacket designed and created by costume designer Jann Paxton. This coat took so long to make that it was finished only days before the opening of the show and long after my illustration was complete. I created my coat for the poster based on a description by Paxton.

tion. The very last thing I drew on the poster was her costume. • I engaged the services of a very talented airbrush illustrator friend, Lu Matthews, to create the title lettering for the poster. We decided to do it in neon, like a marquee. After the neon and sky were completed, Lu decided to add the Hollywood opening night searchlights as a final touch. • A nice marriage between pencil and airbrush. The "coat of many colors" was executed in gouache. • This time everything was spelled right, and the poster really captures the feeling of the musical.

Reference photo of James Hughes. The star of the show, James seemed to come alive in the part only after he had his "coat of many colors." It was not easy to get him to pose for this shot. He was so new to acting that I'm sure all of this just confused him. Here he is posing in a store-bought flight jacket.

Reference photo of Sandee Hayes who played the narrator. We had to shoot Sandee in a bathing suit because the costumer had no idea how he would outfit her for the show. I waited as long as I could before beginning work on her.

nine different colors for the vest, which I drew next. When I drew the pants in pinks, maroon, and orangy vermillions, I knew I was onto something good. Next came the peach suit of the man getting his shoes shined. I was inspired, laboring for hours over the choice of two colors for his striped necktie. I must have tried thirty or forty color combinations.　•　This is probably the first drawing in which the faces are partially hidden, in shadow, or nonexistent, so I paid little attention to the color scheme of the flesh, which became less than secondary.　•　I saved the background for last, unaccustomed to including environments in my drawings. After I got underway on it, the most amazing thing happened. I realized that the figures and the background were essentially on the same plane, so the background comprised a part of the foreground. I liked that. The depth of field had shortened nicely.　　Little dimensionality to the background, few angles, and very little perspective resulted. I was focused in too tight for that. Everything was up front.　•　And another thing occurred. Everything became equally important and interdependent. Another first. Usually I have one main element with everything secondary to it. In this drawing everything came together equally for the first time.

This photo was my reference for *Shoeshine*. As you can see, I took out a lot of extraneous stuff, which left me with a very pleasing composition, all the elements acting and reacting.

Prismacolor pencil on Canson charcoal paper

Mother Of Exiles

The first layout I attempted. This one contains the last and most famous stanza from Emma Lazarus' poem, "The New Colossus." I thought the marriage between the majesty of the statue and the handwriting would create a moving composition. But the client didn't agree.

Next I combined the same image with a grid and a diagrammatic drawing of the hand with the torch. I didn't want to give up the Emma Lazarus poem, but often these things are a series of letdowns and compromises. In this instance, I was doing all the compromising, and they were letting me down.

At last, I received an assignment from a client in New York to illustrate my favorite statue, *Liberty Enlightening the World.* The Statue of Liberty (her American name) is a formidable assignment, to say the least. I knew from the outset that whatever I created would have to pass the review board of the Ellis Island Foundation. But I wasn't concerned. With my respect for this monument to freedom, I knew I just couldn't miss. • Choosing the best approach took some time. I tried various concepts and rejected most of them. My first idea was to incorporate the last, and most famous, lines from Emma Lazarus' poem, "The New Colossus." I found a copy of the original Lazarus manuscript, intending to incorporate her handwritten words into the illustration somehow. I tried many variations of combining the statue with the calligraphy, but none of them jumped out at me. Eventually, the Emma Lazarus poem proved to be too overwhelming, and after numerous attempts to use it, I reluctantly dropped the idea. • There are so many parts of the statue that I like, and yet I knew I couldn't incorporate all of them into the drawing. I had to decide on my favorite part, and, at the same time, to choose a part that would symbolize and embody the idea of Freedom. The hand holding the torch is such a moving image. It represents so much: it's the beacon of light that welcomes; it's the torch of freedom; it says *enlightenment.* I wanted the image in my drawing somehow. And I wanted to use some form of the sculpture in its entirety. So you see, I was making it tough on myself. Yet I knew this was a dream assignment that could represent my personal statement on the power of the national monument. • I guess I always knew I would illustrate the head as my main visual. That head with its almost Art Deco crown is the most powerful aspect of the statue. Naturally, I wanted to capture that

Reference for the schematic of the hand and the torch. These diagrammatic architectural drawings bring out the closet architect in me. Architecture is so important to me, and I like adding these elements to my drawings.

I finally abandoned the foreshortened view of Liberty, when it seemed as if I were going nowhere. So I did more research and developed this drawing. But cutting her right arm off at the shoulder was a mistake, and I couldn't think of what to do with the rest of the drawing.

strength in my drawing. In each design, the statue seemed too small, too lost in the format. I kept thinking, "she's so big," and wanting her to be big in the drawing. I felt the need to focus in close on the head and crown.   •   I started doing layouts of the head, but I noticed I needed something else — the suggestion of the thrust of her raised arm. After adding this, I started to like the drawing, although I still knew something was missing.   •   As I sketched out a layout of this new approach, I decided to fade the detail of the fabric into the background. I liked this. Still, there was something missing, and then it hit me. I wanted to bring the hand with the torch and the whole statue back into the drawing, and the faded area at the bottom seemed the perfect place. I placed the diagrammatic drawing of the hand with the torch in the lower left-hand corner and that instantly decided for me where I would place the stylized drawing of the whole monument. It all worked. And I chose to tie it all together with a grid.   •   With the sketch approved by the client, I started my usual quest for the right paper and the right color scheme. I wanted everything to be warm,

The final version combining all of the elements I like. The pose with the arm raised worked. All I needed was an indication of an arm. The grid seemed to tie it all together. And finally, the small drawings and the addition of the name "Mother of Exiles" made the piece. Or so I thought.

as if bathed by a late afternoon sun. Even though The Statue of Liberty is green, I wanted her to be warmer, without any hint of green. Actually, the warm color of the paper dictated the entire color scheme. All the colors simply had to complement the background color.   •   The procedure went well. I was enthusiastic and enjoyed myself immensely. I was very pleased with the outcome. The drawing had strength and a quiet kind of dignity. The colors worked well. There was an emotional quality to the drawing. I signed it (I always plan out where I sign my name as part of the initial design)

Prismacolor pencil on Crescent mat board/from the collection of Lawyers Title Insurance Co.

Reference photos in post-card form from my swipe files. This is always how I begin. I dig out lots of swipes and then eliminate, and more often than not I come up with a whole new direction. The swipes serve as a jumping off point.

and called Federal Express. • After a few days passed by, I received a phone call from the client telling me that the Ellis Island Foundation had rejected my drawing. The reason? The grid suggested the scaffolding around the statue, and they wanted no reference to the reconstruction process taking place then! And they wanted me to remove the two images at the bottom while I was removing the grid! A double blow. I was shocked. I thought I had done such a nice job. • This once enjoyable project had turned into a nightmare. This drawing became the first illustration I had ever had to do over. It was next to impossible to do it again, especially without its impact and personal emotional statement. But I managed to draw a perfect copy of the drawing…without the heart.

"Keep, ancient lands, your storied pomp!" cries she,
With silent lips. "Give me your tired, your poor,
Your huddled masses yearning to breathe free,
The wretched refuse of your teeming shore,
Send these, the homeless, tempest-tost to me,
I lift my lamp beside the golden door!"

Emma Lazarus.

November 2nd, 1883

Two years before the Statue of Liberty arrived in New York its spirit affected a young Jewish woman named Emma Lazarus so deeply that she felt moved to express her feelings in verse. Over the years, the closing lines of "The New Colossus" would become almost as well-known as the statue it was written to commemorate.

Death Of A Salesman

When you don't live in New York City, or Chicago, or Los Angeles, you have to rely heavily on a delivery service to get the illustration to the destination on time and in one piece. Over the years, I have tried them all and finally found the best: Federal Express. • There are delivery services that can get your drawing to the client the same day you ship it, anywhere in the U.S., for a small fortune. And then there are those slow-boat-to-China shippers that take forever. Naturally, time is a definite factor. Express Mail with the U.S. Post Office guarantees next day service; however, the shipment sometimes reaches its destination as late at 3:30 p.m. the next day, whereas Federal Express guarantees next day delivery by 10:30 a.m. I tried the Eastern Airlines Sprint Service once also. Since that service costs almost as much as it would if I were to fly with the package, I visualized the package occupying a seat in the coach, gazing out the window while being served a continental breakfast. Upon arrival, it had to sit around the airport until someone came to pick it

up. So I'm back to Federal Express, again. They're the best, but they're not perfect. • A case in point — Steve Phillips, a New York magazine designer and old friend, contacted me to do an illustration of Dustin Hoffman as he appeared in the critically acclaimed Broadway play, *Death of a Salesman.* It was a tailor-made assignment for me. I jumped on it with great enthusiasm and in a few days it was complete. Steve needed it by a certain date, and I had worked up to the day the drawing was due in New York City. At last, I picked up the phone and said, "Hello Federal." I wish I hadn't. I wish, in this instance, I had let Dustin Hoffman look out the window on the plane while sipping his gin and tonic. Federal Express lost the package! I know it's unheard of, but nevertheless, the drawing vanished! • When an art director calls to tell you he hasn't received the package, that's devastating news enough. But when it comes from a friend who suffers from grave misconceptions concerning communication and transportation systems anywhere outside of New York, that's ten times worse. Once, many years ago, when I was leaving Richmond on an Eastern Airlines flight to New York City to work with Steve, my plane hit a deer on the runway and had to return to the hangar for

damage inspection. We were delayed about forty-five minutes. When I finally arrived at Steve's and told him what had happened, he didn't seem all that surprised. He informed me that he imagined Richmond, Virginia was overrun with wildlife, anyway, and he wasn't surprised in the least that we hit a deer. I fear that most New York art directors believe there is a time gap between them and the rest of the world outside of New York, making it impossible for them to get anything on time—a gap in years, I mean. They believe modern ways haven't reached us yet; we just got "talkies" last week.   •   I had finally convinced Steve that his misconceptions had no basis in reality, so it was just my luck that Federal Express had to spoil its perfect record with me and lose a package going to Steve Phillips. I feel certain that the minute it was late, he reverted back to some past prejudice. Steve probably had a vision of Federal Express here in Richmond working out of a log cabin with wagons and horses for deliveries and pickups!   •   My investigation of Dustin Hoffman's fate began by calling Federal. They first gave me a control number, and then they instigated a trace. A few hours later, I breathed a slight sigh of relief when they informed me the package had arrived in time in New

York and had been sidetracked somewhere in that area. At least the blame wasn't on Federal in Richmond — the horse and wagon services of Federal Express in Manhattan had lost it. Alas, that still didn't bring me any closer to finding it. I kept calling Federal, and they kept asking me for my control number. I kept giving it to them, and they kept continually giving me the impression they thought their system worked because they could punch my control number in their computer to discover there was nothing new to report on Dustin Hoffman. This, however, did not convince me that their system worked. Obviously, there was a breakdown somewhere. • Now Federal Express is great, and their television commercials are great, but they have one major problem: when they lose something, there is no one higher-up with whom to register a complaint when you are dissatisfied with what's taking place at entry level. I tried. There isn't even a number in the phone book for anyone else. I couldn't locate any executive offices, only dispatchers and control numbers, and nothing was getting done. • Finally, one dispatcher connected me with a dispatcher in New York. Bright guy that he was, his records showed the package had been delivered that morning. Exasperated, I called Steve and asked him to check all over the building, but to no avail. Now I was desperate. After finally getting through to Federal Express in New York, I found they thought they had delivered it. Great. • The next morning, after I had spent a totally nonproductive day with dispatchers and control numbers, New York Federal Express called to say that it had just been delivered. I couldn't rest with their word alone, so I called Steve. It was true. I was very relieved. • When I saw the drawing in print some weeks later, I noticed that Dustin Hoffman's hair was a lot whiter than I had originally drawn it. This was no great surprise. Federal Express had added a few gray hairs to my head, also.

Prismacolor pencil, airbrush on Crescent mat board

The Designer

I always think of one word when I think of Ken Cook...
perfection. Not a perfectionist, someone battling away at an
all too imperfect world to no avail. Perfection, the possible
and achievable perfection caused by a thorough understand-
ing of his talents and his craft. • In an era when
words such as *graphic* and *design* are all too commonly
used, Ken is a true graphic designer. The title fits him well.
He possesses an overview that enables him to solve design
problems seemingly with ease. I know differently (I know
how hard he worked on this book). But the outcome is so
seamless that it appears to have just happened in an in-
stant. • Ken is also a dreamer. But he has no illusions
about his limitations. He dreams dreams that he can make
happen. He plans and executes his dreams like a design
problem. • This book is a tribute to his talents. — *Bill*